AF265437

Destined to Win

Breaking Through Obstacles in Life

Dr. L'Tanya James

Table Of Contents

Dedication

Acknowledgement

Introduction

What Others are Saying

Dedication

I dedicate this book to men and women who have experienced struggles in life.

To those of you who have had other people to try to block, stop, sabotage, derail or attempt to get you off course from your purpose.

I dedicate this book to hurting people who feel like you cannot go on another day, but you can and you will, because if I can do it, then so can you!

Acknowledgement

I would like to first acknowledge my husband, Terry James of thirty-two years of marriage, at the publishing of this book. For his love, support, encouragement, and for standing by my side as a woman in ministry, and allowing me to be free to go forth, and do what God has called me to do!

I love you baby!

To my children, Deant'e & Sharayah James, and my daughter-in-law, Natacha James; for their love, support, and encouragement in the process of me writing this book.

To my spiritual parents and pastors: Dr. Fred and Pastor Linda Hodge of Living Praise Christian Center, one church in three locations, who mentored me and caused me to stretch and go to another dimension; with my walk with the Lord, and develop and bring forth skills within me to come forth and produce live-changing results!

To my parents: Matthew W. Thomas & Ella Marie Thomas, who were the best parents that anyone could ever ask for. They imparted into me that I can do anything and have everything that I desire and are believing for in life! Who modeled before me what a Godly marriage looks like for 61 years and how I can have a good marriage as well.

Introduction

Take a journey with me through the pages of this book. Discover how you are destined to win in life!

All of us undergo numerous transitions; career changes, moving to new locations, starting different relationships, recent births or deaths, accomplishments, promotions, disappointments and trials. Nevertheless, we win through Jesus Christ! Just like the Apostle Paul endured countless obstacles, he remained a winner.

Romans 8:35-39 NLT says, "Can anything ever separate us from Christ's love? Does it mean He no longer loves us if we have trouble or calamity, or are persecuted, or are hungry or cold or in danger or threatened with death?" As the Scriptures say, "For your sake we are killed every day; we are being slaughtered like sheep. No, despite, all these things, overwhelming victory is ours through Christ, who loved us. And I am convinced that nothing can ever separate us from his love. Death can't. The Angels can't and the demons can't. Our fears for today, our worries about tomorrow, and even the powers of hell can't keep God's love away. Whether we are high above the sky or in deepest ocean, nothing in all creation will ever be able to separate us from the love of God that is revealed in Christ Jesus our Lord."

We are more than conquers through Christ that strengthens us. You see, despite everything that we encounter, Jesus is at the right hand of God praying for us, and cheering us on, assuring us that we can make it and cross the finish line victoriously (Hebrews 7:25).

What Others are Saying

Dr. L'Tanya James is a unique woman of God full of faith and power. She exemplifies kingdom leadership through her humility, inner strength, and transparency. Her love for God's people is evident in the compassionate way she responds to those whom she serves. Through practical application of the scripture, coupled with her unyielding faith, she has overcome the obstacles faced in her personal and professional life. Dr. L'Tanya is a dynamic teacher, intercessor, and conference speaker with a passion to reach the lost. This book will both inspire and encourage you, as you receive revelation on how to take hold of the promises of God. And, by faith persevere until victory is a reality. I am truly honored to know this exceptional woman of God.

Elder Doneita Harmon

Dr. L'Tanya is, as the Apostle Paul would say, "a living epistle being read of men." She communicates the Gospel through teaching and preaching with a passion that will galvanize people into believing and pursuing God's best. Her fervor behind the pulpit is matched by her compassion and nurturing spirit that is necessary for lasting impact and maturity.

Pastor Fred J. Burns, II

Dynamic, strong, faithful, and anointed. These are words that describe this woman of God, who has been a watchman on the wall to this generation. As a co-laborer in the ministry, Dr. L'Tanya James has watered my dry moments with her faith and planted new hope with encouraging words. I am honored to call her friend.

Minister Keven Farmer

Chapter 1
Excess in the Trunk

Have you ever opened the trunk of your car after going to the grocery store, only to discover that your trunk was cluttered? You found a stroller, blankets, clothes, empty water bottles, and other items. This clutter was piling up for the past few weeks. Of course, there was a time when each piece had a destination such as; the cleaners, thrift store, recycle center, and possibly dumpster? But now, you find yourself haphazardly rearranging your trunk in order to fit your groceries.

It's the same when we haven't cleared the clutter out of our lives. In order to receive the word of God, we must free up space. According to Romans 12:2 (New Spirit-Filled Life Bible, NLT) says, "And do not be conformed to this world, but be transformed by the renewing of your mind that you may prove what is that good and acceptable and perfect will of God." Like King David cried out to the Lord in Psalms 51, "Create in me a clean heart, O God and renew a steadfast spirit within me."

In life we, face countless circumstances. Oftentimes, those extenuating situations cause us to accumulate excess weight on our heart, which requires cleansing. In this way, God can place what He wants in our heart, and remove what may hinder the new information such as; "we are more than conquers through Christ Jesus that strengthens us," and "God does not give us the spirit of fear, but of power, love, and a sound mind." It is unfortunate that due to the negative words that have been spoken over us, we sometimes settle for less than what God has for us. It is imperative to forgive people that have offended us, maligned our character, and tried to impede our progress and self-worth. In all actuality, they have really helped to catapult us to a bigger and higher level.

I remember a time when my pastor asked me to start a prison ministry for the church. I began researching all the aspects of prison ministry: the criteria, and what to expect. Thus, I found an organization that trained all the volunteers to be effective. Everyone was trained. It was approximately 30 or so volunteers in the program. Then, we had one more step, which was to be officially processed.

When the chaplain in charge of the volunteers discovered I was a woman, he was livid! He couldn't believe I was in charge of men and women, plus implementing a powerful prison ministry. The chaplain was angry because he was attached to a denomination that said women can't lead other men or hold any leadership positions. Can you believe he devised a plan that would sabotage my church leadership position, along with those who represented my church, as volunteers under my supervision?

As life would have it, I didn't realize the chaplain's underhanded efforts until later. Finally, the day arrived when my church volunteer and I were set to meet inmates for the first time. A church volunteer from another ministry brought in a Billy Graham Crusade video, and played it for the inmates. I led Bible study and they were receptive of our presentation. A couple of days passed, and we didn't hear anything from the prison. Before the week's end, I received a call that my clearance to visit and minister was revoked. Why? The chaplain didn't clear the Billy Graham video the inmates watched. I explained to the chaplain that I did not bring the video. Nor, was I the person that played the video. But, the chaplain did not believe me. What's more, the chaplain allowed the other volunteer to continue visiting and ministering to the inmates. I was devastated. I couldn't figure out how and why this could happen to me. I knew I was called to lead a prison ministry. Nothing could deter me from the vision. I fasted and prayed, seeking God's answer as to where I went wrong.

One thing's for sure. I was lied on and treated unfairly because I was a woman. At the same time, people from other churches learned what happened and shared information about ministering in youth detention camps. But, the chaplain at Challenger Memorial Detention

Center heard about my experience. And, God gave me favor with the man of God.

That chaplain trained me in the administrative functioning of prison ministry. Within a short period of time, I went through the process and was cleared. Thus, began my journey in prison ministry at Challenger Memorial Detention Center.

The head chaplain granted me special clearance, where all I had to do was swipe my card to enter. I didn't have to go through a long special security gate entrance. The chaplain gave me an office and proceeded to train me in prison ministry. At that particular time, I went in all the camps and was allowed to attend all the services. Crips, Bloods, and every other gang was attended the same Sunday service, which potentially could have been very dangerous. There were no peace treaties: Fights could have broken out at any time. But, they didn't due to the presence of God was at every service. God was glorified. As the Lord used me to minister to the youth; not one incident occurred. There was an out pouring of God's Spirit in those services, where hard-core gang bangers would cry and weep in the presence of the Lord! Now, what if I allowed offense and hurt to enter my heart? What if I didn't allow the Lord to minister to me? Would I have ministered to the youth? No! I would've missed a tremendous opportunity to minister to all those teenage inmates.

I would like for you to meditate on your life from this point to where you are today. Do you remember a time when you prayed and believed God for something and it didn't happen? You wondered where you went wrong. You created multiple checklists asking, "Am I walking in unforgiveness toward someone?"

Then, you discover that all along, God had something better for you than what you initially thought was best for you. Now, when you look back in retrospect, you thank God for not giving you what you wanted. God knows what's best for each and every one of us He knows the whole picture before we see the manifestation of it. I once heard a story about a man of God that was close to his retirement, but he came across another job that he felt was a better fit for him. The job supposedly had more money and brighter opportunities. The man who applied for the job, prayed, declared the job was his, then spoke the word over it, and expected to receive it. A bit of time transpired until human resources told the man that he did not get the job. He was shocked because he did all the "right things."

Once again, he prayed and believed God that he would receive it. He quoted all the scriptures, yet he still wasn't hired. Several weeks went by, and a scandal broke across the news involving this very same company. The scandal not only rocked the company, but was the cause of it being shut down. Had the believer decided to go with the new company, he would've lost all his retirement, medical benefits, 401K, and everything he had acquired during the past 30 years. God knows all and sees what is coming, so be encouraged. God has your back. He has something better in store for you. Or, He is also protecting you from something down the road that you don't see.

Chapter 2
Purpose

When we refer to Webster's dictionary, we find the definition for purpose: *"An intended or desired result: goal. 2. Determination: resolve. To intend to do: resolve. Purposeful."*

During the time of conception in our mother's womb, God had a plan and a purpose for our lives. He knew our skin color and gender, down to the date and time of every birth. God even knew each and every one of our parents! It doesn't matter if you were planned in your parent's eyes or not. The fact is that God has a plan and a purpose for you!

Psalms 139:14 (New Spirit-Filled Life Bible, NLT) says:

"I will praise you, for I am fearfully and wonderfully made. Marvelous are your works, and that my soul knows very well." God does not make any junk! You are special: you are someone in Christ who's <u>Destined to Win!</u>

When you visit the store to make a purchase, its cover usually displays the contents of the package. Say we're shopping for a swing set for a child or grandchild. We see one that we like and read the box. It says, "2-in-1 Swing & Rocker, 16 songs with 2 sounds." The product sounds appealing and the price is affordable. You purchase the swing, get home, open it up, and learn that the song feature does not work.

So here's the question. Do you go to a manufacturer down the street, who did not design that product but is cheaper just for your own convenience? Or, do you go to the manufacturer that designed it? Most would go to the manufacturer of that product.

It is the same principle if you own a Mercedes. You don't take it to a BMW dealer to service it. Take it to the Mercedes dealer and get it serviced. Why? Mercedes dealers produced the vehicle and know why it functions. They are able to diagnose any problems by the performance of your vehicle.

Genesis 1:26-28 (New Spirit-Filled Bible, NLT), verse 26, "And God said, let us make man in our image according to our likeness, let them have dominion over the fish of the sea, over the birds of the air, and over the cattle, over all the earth and over every creeping thing that creeps on the earth." Verse 27, "So God created man in his own image; in the image of God He created him; male and female He created them." Verse 28, Then God blessed them, and God said, to them, "Be fruitful and multiply, fill the earth and subdue it; have dominion over the fish of the sea, over the birds of the air, and over every living thing that moves on the earth."

God is the one who created us. We are created after His image and after His likeness. We have His DNA running in our veins. He did not make any rejects. We are wonderfully and fearfully made by God (Psalms 139:14).

Today when a car is wrecked, the results are typically costly! A manufacturer will total out the car with conclusions that damages are more costly than the car is worth. On the contrary, with God you may have been damaged by life's irreparable issues; rejection, abuse, shortcomings and past mistakes. Thankfully, God is the one who repairs the shattered pieces in your life which we will discuss in our next chapter. Think about it. God created you and me for a purpose.

There was a reason why we were born. Purpose is something that you love, something that you flow in without hesitation, or any hard effort. You think about your purpose all the time, and you are ready to do it at any given moment of the day. Purpose is a burning passion inside of you, where you know, "This is something I need to do." It makes you joyful. While fulfilling your purpose, it blesses others as they partake of your fruit. Purpose brings expansion in your life. Purpose brings vision: purpose brings favor in what God has told you to do. Purpose brings increase.

I have a question for you. Are you walking in purpose right now? If not, go back to your manufacturer (God) to discover your purpose.

Then, walk purposefully after revelation. God knows every intricate part of you: He even knows the numbers of hair on your head (Matthew 10:30). Our Heavenly Father knows everything about us! This is a revelatory moment. God knows what you are going to do before you do it. Can you imagine that? He also knows what you are going to say before you speak. God intensely loves us. However, He has given everyone a free will to obey or disobey Him.

King Saul was instructed by the prophet of God, Samuel, to attack the Amalekites. They lived in Canaan's southern desert land. King Saul was told to utterly destroy the Amalekites by neither sparing them nor their property.

Man and woman, infant and nursing child, ox and sheep, camel and donkey (1 Samuel 15:1-7). Verse 8 states, "He also took Agag, King of Amalek alive, and utterly destroyed all the people with the edge of the sword. Verse 9 says, "But Saul and the people spared Agag and the best of the sheep, the oxen, the fatlings, the lambs, and all that was good, and were unwilling to utterly destroy them. But everything despised and worthless, that's what they destroyed."

1 Samuel 15:10 says, "Now the word of the Lord came to Samuel, saying I greatly regret that I have set up Saul as king. For he has turned back from following me, and has not performed my commandments.' And it grieved Samuel, and he cried out to the Lord all night."

God already knew how Saul was going to act. The conclusion of the story: Saul was deceived by altering the instructions and making an excuse to Samuel. The prophet told Saul to be quiet and listen to God's full instructions. Verse 17, "Then Samuel said to Saul, when you were little in your own eyes, were you not head of the tribes of Israel? And did not the Lord anoint you king over Israel?" Verse 18 says, "Now the Lord sent you on a mission, and said, 'Go, and utterly destroy the sinners, the Amalekites and fight against them until they are consume.'" Verse 19 says, "Why then, did you not obey the voice of the Lord? Why did you swoop down on the spoil, and do evil in the sight of the Lord?" Verse 20 says, "And Saul said to Samuel, but I have obeyed the voice of the Lord, and gone on the mission on which the Lord sent me, and brought back Agag, King of Amalek; I have utterly destroyed the Amalekites."

Verse 21, (Saul blames the people for what he did and he was the leader.)   Verse 22-23 states, "So Samuel said has the Lord as great delight in burnt offerings and sacrifices as in obeying the voice of the Lord? Behold to obey is better than sacrifice, and to heed than the fat of rams." Verse 23 says, "For rebellion is as the sin of witchcraft, and stubbornness is as iniquity and idolatry. Because you have rejected the word of the Lord, He also has rejected you from being king."

Saul got fired because he did not obey God. Our Heavenly Father had a plan and purpose for Saul. Just like God has a plan for all of us. But, by Saul's own volition, he added his own instructions and reasons for deciding his own way was better. King Saul's example should remind us all to obey and seek God for guidance. It's the only way to avoid trouble.

Chapter 3

Shattered and Put Back Together

I distinctly recall January 18, 2011, as an unusually cold day. I was more apprehensive than normal about visiting my dentist. The thought of seeing the dentist always triggered mild discomfort, along with feeling some slight pain. I was thinking of what I needed to accomplish that day. I wondered, what I was going to be ministering on to thousands of radio listeners, tuning in later. I pulled into the parking lot, where my dental office was located. As I approached a parking space, I looked down on the ground. A broken glass was shattered into numerous pieces. Instantly, the Lord spoke and directed me to share this powerful revelation on that day's radio broadcast.

God told me to remember how I, too, was first shattered like that broken glass. I was 16 years-old, and have always been the type of person with compassion for the underdogs – those that were teased or bullied. I knew a particular young man that was bullied. He wasn't very handsome, and girls really didn't pay him too much attention. Sadly, nobody wanted to go with him to the prom. I felt sorry for him and told him that I would be his date. He picked me up for the prom and I had on my debutante dress, which was a wedding dress with a big hoop slip underneath like Scarlet O'Hara's.

We enjoyed the festivities of the prom and it was time to go home. On the drive home, I started noticing unfamiliar territory. I thought to myself, "This doesn't look like the way to my home." The boy drove slightly faster through the mountains as the road was becoming more steep and narrower. By now, I was deeply concerned because it finally hit me that he really wasn't taking me home!

Finally, we stopped, pulled on the side of the winding road, and he tried to make me to have sex with him. But, I jumped out of the car and walked as fast as my heels could take me in the dark mountains, down the steep, narrow hill. Keep in mind; I was wearing a debutante dress with hoop under it. So, it was very difficult to walk. "For He shall give His angels charge over you" (NKJV-Psalm 91:11). My heart was racing, I thought, "What am I going do?" I took off my hoop so I could walk better.

I was frightened! It was 1974. There were no cell phones, and there sure wasn't a pay phone in the mountains. Somehow, my prom date talked me into getting back in his car. Why? Blame it on my heels and the steep, dark mountains. He drove some more and went to a residential area in Granada Hills, Calif. He attempted to try to rape me again! But he couldn't. This time, I jumped out of the car and ran to a white house; it was around one o'clock in the morning. I banged on the door and rung the doorbell.

A man approached the door and asked, "Who is it?" I said, "L'Tanya. I call my mom and Dad?" He pulled open the curtain that draped the glass door and let me in, while locking the door behind us. He asked me what happened and I told him. About five minutes passed and the guy who took me to the prom banged on the door, trying to get me. Can you believe that? The nice man, who let me in his house to use the phone, told my date that if he didn't get away from the door, he was going to blow him away. I thought, "Wow this is a stranger protecting me!" The nice stranger later told me that he, too, had daughters and would want someone to do the same.

My parents picked me up and thanked the nice man. God had His hands on me even before I knew Him. He protected me. God was and remains my constant and steadfast deliverer.

Let's return to the story about the broken glass on the ground. God revealed this to me:

A shattered piece of glass is broken into innumerable, diverse pieces. Through the natural eye, those pieces appear like they can never be put back together.

But on the contrary – it's not true with God. In Him, all things are possible. For you see there are many of you out there, just like me who have been shattered into a million of pieces. Some are shattered by abusive husbands who beat you physically or mentally by their insulting words. Many put you down and make you feel like life isn't worth living. Others are shattered by abusive wives: you know women can be verbally abusive with their mouths by mistreating their husbands and making them feel less than a man.

All too many are shattered by a loss of jobs. People have lost their jobs due to layoffs, being fired, or other circumstances that have impacted their income. Far too many are shattered by the death of a loved one, who died suddenly or transitioned over a period of time. Numerous are shattered by broken dreams. Future plans that you started out to achieve are placed on hold a shelf in your mind because of life's adversities. But stick to the course. Hebrews 11:1 (NIV) says, "Now faith is confidence in what we hope for and assurance about what we do not see."

God has given me a word for you this day. El ROI, "The God Who Sees." The God, who sees me, is the same God who sees you. And He says, *"He is putting back the pieces in your life that have been shattered: My son, my daughter, you thought that this was it. Oh, no! My child, this is not it!*

For there is more to the more that I have in store for you! More opened doors, more favor that I have in store for you.

You thought that this was it and that you were going under. I said, "No! Not so, my child. I have prepared you for such a time as this to represent me in the earth.

I have equipped you and called you to go and fulfill your assignment. Go to the places, where I have called you. For this year, I am moving and touching the lives of the backslider and the unsaved alike.

As I heal you, and put you back together, and make you whole, you will minister, and bring healing to others that have been shattered and broken by life's issues."

There was a time when I literally felt the pain that so many of you have experienced. It was as if I was undergoing the suffering upon myself. I felt the pain of the single mother, who was alone raising her children without support from the father. Why? You may ask, because

I felt what my very own daughter experienced in her life. One day, as I was on my computer my daughter sat on the floor behind me and told me, "Mom I need to talk to you." She stated she was pregnant. I wasn't surprised because the Lord informed me a week or so before my daughter told me. I listened and then I told my daughter that her father and I would be there for her. She already knew what she had done was wrong because she grew up in a Christian home and knew the word.

Yes, I am a minister and we dealt with this together as a family. When people would ask I didn't try to hide it. My daughter confronted an array of emotional battles as a single parent, learning how to provide for her son. God is a forgiving God. He is the God of second chances. Yes, you can make it! Life isn't easy when you are in ministry, especially when your child or children make decisions that don't line up with the word of God. Shake it off and lock in with God, He will bring you through the pain.

As a prayer intercessor, sometimes, I know how it feels when I'm standing in the gap, taking prayers to the Lord! I endured the anguish of a woman whose husband left her for another woman. I felt the hurt of the mother praying for her wayward child abusing drugs.

Several hours passed and it was time to record on the radio broadcast. The radio host, Melvin Slade, introduced me to the audience. God's almighty power, as well as, the presence of the Holy Spirit rested upon me. I started declaring what God told me to share through revelation. It was a powerful broadcast! God had orchestrated the whole message, and He had a special word for the listeners that day. God can speak to us in numerous different ways. It's important that we're sensitive to His promptings, even when going about everyday tasks. God is always speaking to us.

You shouldn't remain stuck in difficult situations, or insurmountable challenges. Seek God your Creator.

God knows us better than we know ourselves: He knows what He has created and destined for you. God will take everything that you've encountered in life, and apply it toward your purpose and plan to create your best future. Never give up. You see it is right at that time when the pressure is so strong that you give up. Why? Because it's an easy thing to do. Don't do it. You are almost there! That's why the pressure seems insurmountable because you are near the finish line. Press yourself to the other side of victory. Walk in the promise that God has destined for you and me. There are many illustrations in the Bible of people who were in situations for a long period of time. However, there was an *"and suddenly"* moment that happened in their life and it forever changed their circumstance! Let's look at what happen to Mephibosheth.

Mephibosheth was Jonathan's son and King Saul's grandson.2 Samuel 9:1-12 (New Spirit-Filled Bible, NLT) says, "Now David said, 'Is there still one who is left of the house of Saul, that I may show him kindness for Jonathan's sake.' David and Jonathan were very close and like brothers. They had made a vow with each other." 1Samuel 20:42 (New Spirit-Filled Bible, NLT) says, "Then Jonathan said to David go in peace, since we both sworn in the name of the Lord, saying May the Lord be between you and me and between your descendants and my descendants, forever."

1Samuel 9:2 (New Spirit-Filled Bible, NLT) says, "And there was a servant of the Saul whose name was Ziba. So when they called him David, the king said to him, are you Ziba? He said at your service. Verse 3 says, "Then the king said, is there not still someone of the house of Saul, to whom I may show the kindness of God? And Ziba said to the king. There is still a son of Jonathan who is lame in his feet." Verse 4 says, "So the king said to him, where is he? And Ziba said to the king, indeed, he is in the house of Machir the son of Ammiel, in Lo Debar."

A great number of you reading this book are at Lo Debar, figuratively speaking. You are at the right place to receive what God has intended for you to possess. You see, during this moment, Mephibosheth was at a very low state in his life. When he was very young, Mephibosheth's nurse dropped and crippled him. Machir, a wealthy man, took Mephibosheth into his home as an orphan. Ziba, one of Machir's servants took care of Mephibosheth. You may not have physical challenges, but you may have been crippled by life's circumstances. Or, you're paralyzed by the fear of stepping out again. Maybe, you've developed low self- esteem just like Mephibosheth (1 Samuel 9:8). He was beat down so bad that he called himself a dead dog. Look up to where cometh your help, our help comes from above. You are a winner in Christ, and after all the dust settles you are still standing. The outcome of this story is victorious.

Ziba, the servant took care of Mephibosheth, per instructions by King David in how he and his sons were going to work the land. The harvest of the fruit would go to Mephibosheth for him to eat. From now on, Mephibosheth would eat at the king's table forever as like one of the king's sons. Mephibosheth had a change in his life. Be encouraged your due season is here for some of you, and to others it's on its way. God is faithful! He has not forgotten about you. God is a God to the fatherless. He is a healer to those who need healing. He is a way, where there is no way. He is peace to those who need peace. He is joy to those who need joy this day. Praise Him for He is worthy to receive Praise!

Chapter 4

In His Manifested Presence

Are you at a place in your walk with the Lord that you must be in the constant presence of the Lord: steadily spending time with Him, ministering to Him and Him ministering to you? You see, remaining regularly in the Lord's presence means you're able to clearly His voice and direction for your life and things that are to come.

From July 18-20Th in 2008, I held a women's conference. The title of the conference was, *"In His Manifested Presence."* I went before the Lord and asked Him where the location would be and He directed me to the San Bernardino Mountains. It was 6,000 feet-high, and far away from cell phones getting reception and distractions. The ladies that attended had an expectant heart to receive everything that God had for them including myself. Early in the morning, we walked up a path along the mountain that led to Chapel Hill for prayer. The climb wasn't too steep. It was a nice, cool walk before the weather turned scorching later that afternoon. From Chapel Hill, it was a picturesque view of the San Bernardino Mountains.

We went before the Father in prayer and He manifested Himself to all that attended. The Holy Spirit manifested Himself with a gentle brush of air that gently swept across the faces of many that were there. Women wept from the presence of the Lord. You see, when you're truly thirsty for the Lord and hungry to be before Him, and minister to Him, He will show up. The Lord wants us to come to Him, and worship Him in spirit and in truth. He wants us to love Him more than anything in this world. The Lord wants us to come before Him, and rid ourselves from all distractions that are around us. He wants all of us. If God asks you to get rid of all distractions in your life would you? Would you be willing to sacrifice it all? Would you be willing to sacrifice the so-called friends that you have in your inner circle who are really hindrances to you and not assets to you in your destiny?

Are you willing to get rid of that extra job that has preoccupied so much of your free time, that you don't have time for God any more. It could even be activities in your life that have you so booked up, that you don't have time for God. What's even more detrimental is wasting your time doing nothing all day and accomplishing nothing.

Talking on the phone all day, in which is a waste of time. I know there are many of you who still work a nine to five. However, there still has to be a set time to spend before the Creator of heaven and earth. Spending time before the Father will manifest His presence in your life.

There have been times when I walk in a place and have been told that they can feel God's presence on me. That comes from being in God's presence. When I was working on a full time job I would take my lunch break and go to the park and spend time with God. I had a strong desire to separate myself and spend time with Him. Even to this day, I am not a clique-oriented person; I prefer to be alone. Yes, I fellowship with others quite often, but in a general sense, I love spending time alone with my Daddy, Abba, Father.

I have learned in life that there will be people in your life for a season, some short, and others longer, and even some for a lifetime. But, we must learn from those relationships, and ask the Father why He has brought certain people into your life. And if there are others that have come into your life and are not of God, ask God to reveal them to you so that you can eradicate them from your life.

Allow God to direct your steps in relationships with others. He knows those that are best for you and the ones that He has specifically ordained you to establish relationships.

Staying before the Father will keep you on track
with destiny for your life.

Chapter 5

Pitfalls Designed to Sabotage Your Destiny

Have you ever experienced a time where you were making great momentum in your walk with the Lord: when out of nowhere an individual attached themselves to you. Maybe, you were at an all-time low in your life. You may have just lost a loved one from a sudden death or possibly a terminal illness that you watched them deteriorate before your very eyes. It could have been the betrayal of your husband or wife: you were on the frontline in ministry, Pastor over a thriving church, when everything that was hidden in the dark was suddenly exposed; and due to you're being in a vulnerable state from being hit with so much devastation, it seemed like your guard and spiritual discernment was at an all-time low and unaware to you the devil slipped in one of his agents to draw you off-course from the plan and purposes of God for your life. Let me share with you a story that actually happened so that you can learn and not make the same mistakes that I did.

In February 2011, my mother had a stroke, leaving her paralyzed on her right side, and also taking her speech. She required 24-hr care and was transferred from the hospital to a convalescent hospital. Eventually, my mom was transferred to me to offer caregiver services until I could interview and look at prospective boarding care homes. This was a very challenging task, due to single-handedly carrying the load. My sister lived in Oakland and my brother did not have transportation to help me. I went to see my mother daily, and ensured she was well taken care of until her passing on April 21, 2011 at the age of 88 years-old.

My mother was an elegant, dignified, and classy woman of God. I also viewed her as a Proverbs 31 woman. As a result of my mother's passing and all the work that was left on me to finalize things, I was physically and mentally drained. This woman who I had known for 20 years, started to befriend me and act like she really was concerned about my well-being. She also planted seeds into my ear on how she mentors people in their kingdom authority. It sounded OK to me. What could be wrong about that? This woman who we will call Mollie, which is not her actual name, asked to meet me at Panera Bread for a time of fellowship. So, I consented. By the end of our fellowship time, I had asked her to mentor me and it was the worst decision I'd ever made. This woman was very knowledgeable of the word. Remember, Satan knows the word as well Matthew 4:1-11 says:

"When Jesus was led up by the Spirit into the wilderness to be tempted by the devil. And when He had fasted forty days and forty nights, afterward He was hungry." Now when the tempter came, he said, "If you are the Son of God, command that these stones become bread." But He answered and said, "It is written, Man shall not live by bread alone, but by every word that proceeds from the mouth of God." Then the devil took him up into the holy city, set him on the pinnacle of the temple, and said to Him, "If you are the Son of God, throw yourself down, For it is written: He shall give His angels charge over you, and in their hands they shall bear you up

lest you dash your foot against a stone." The devil quoted straight from Psalms 91, but Jesus always came back with what is written.

Please don't be deceived listen to the promptings, warnings, and red flags that are standing and staring you right in the face!

The following are some of the red flags that I witnessed:

1. Take note to individuals that are not submitted to God-given authority or anyone else in authority.

2. Ask them the question, "What church do you go to?" A person who operates under a false spirit will say I am not a member of any church, and will refuse to get connected.

3. They will place themselves and rank themselves over you in superiority and try to cause you to fear even questioning them in what they say. Your fear is not a fear as in being scared but it's a reverent

fear out of respect because in actuality you have so much Holy Spirit in you that you want to show respect to those whom you *"think"* are sent by God. However, everything no matter whom they say they are; must line up with the word of God and be of sound doctrine.

4. Beware of someone who when you share with them that God spoke to you, and they refute it by saying, "You didn't hear from God, but this is in fact what He is saying."

5. When someone asks you for money for them mentoring you, and says that they haven't worked in years because God told them not to work: but instead they manipulate others to financially support their work, yet will not submit to anybody, flee!

6. They will plant suggestions into your mind as if they were your own decisions when in fact they are not. You are being manipulated to do the enemies plan and agenda.

This escapade lasted for one year. My dear brother and sister, it is very important that you know your destiny and purpose in life. Because if you allow trauma and trials to cause you to put down your guard and be open to people who operate in a jezebel spirit to attach themselves to you, it could possibly get you off course for a season and for some, if they don't listen to the warnings of the Spirit of God it could possibly get you off track for longer than you would like to be.

Always stay connected to your pastors and communicate with them all of your endeavors.

By me going on a week's fast and praying, I was able to hear God clearly in this matter and was delivered from the plan the enemy had set for me. Know your purpose in life and know your destiny!

Prophetic Word

God is getting ready to take some of you this year to another dimension in your ministry.

A momentum shift is occurring right now. You were in the back and God is bringing you in the front.

Ministry doors are opened to you: calls are coming to invite you to speak at conferences, meetings and rallies, get your calendars out for some of you they will begin to fill up this year!

Chapter 6
Destined to Win

Destined- *to appoint to any purpose or end; as, he was destined for the ministry. To settle in advance; foreordained; as his hopes were destined to be realized.*

~Winston Dictionary for Schools.

Man and woman of God, God has set you apart, He has foreordained, settled in advance for you and through you to walk in your destiny and purpose, for your destiny and purpose will surely come to pass in your life and will be a reality not only to you but, others that are around you. Jerimiah1:5.

Have you ever had this conversation with yourself, that there was more to your life than what you were experiencing right now? I know because I have been there, too. In a season of my life, I felt within me that there was more to the more of God's assignment for me. So I began to go more before God, and He began to UN fold His will for me and for my life.

Let's take some time and deal with women who have been called into the fivefold ministry: Apostle, Prophet, Evangelist, Pastor, and Teacher. That's right God is not a respecter of person's. News flash: God *has* called women, too!

Galatians 4:28 (NLT) says, "There is no longer Jew or Gentile, slave or free, male or female. For you are all Christians, you are one in Christ."

Acts 10:34 (NLT) says, "Then Peter replied, I see very clearly that God doesn't show partiality."

Unfortunately we still have some ministers and laity alike who feel that women have their place in ministry and it is not in the pulpit.

We can look back into history and see many women of God who went forth in ministry regardless of what anyone else said or thought.

Mary Woodworth Etter, a powerful evangelist in the 1800's who obeyed God when it was not very popular for a woman to preach and when she did, thousands were saved, healed, and delivered in her tent meetings.

Aimee Simple McPherson, The founder of the four square church defied all odds that were set against her. She overcame all limitations from being a woman and affected millions for the Lord.

Katherine Kulman, was a powerful evangelist in the '70s, where signs, wonders, and miracles were manifested in her meetings.

This is just a small portion of women who were used by God. Let me emphasize women are not just called to evangelize and teach Sunday school! They are called also as Apostles, Prophets, Pastors, and Teachers, too. Yes, I said Pastor too! There were many women ostracized when they stepped forward and said God has called them to pastor or that they were called as a Prophetess. I have seen women who got the left foot of fellowship because they were a Prophetess and many women have been called Jezebels and controllers when they were not weak women but instead knew who they were in Christ. We are in a new season now; God has not been pleased with this kind of mistreatment to His daughters. God is rising up women Apostles, Prophetess, Evangelist, Pastors and Teachers in this last day.

His daughters shall minister to the Nations and declare what saith the Lord! God is rising up women Pastors who will pastor mega churches! That's right women will pastor mega churches, and nothing will be held back from them. God is speaking to you woman of God. What has He told you to do? Stop settling for less because of past tradition. God has called you woman of God. Just do it! Push back all the barriers, push off the limitations: renew your mind of who you are in God.

"You are destined to win and you are a winner." God is raising powerful women of God who will work side-by-side with mighty men of God. Together, they will do damage to the kingdom of darkness.

Are you one of those women who will say yes? Or, are you a woman that someone has told you, "Because you are a woman stay in your place?" It's time for you to rise up woman of God and be the mighty woman that God has called you to be! Don't settle for less than what God has told you. It is sad when others try to intimidate you by calling you names in order for you to cower down to them. But say to yourself, "It's too late. I already know who I am in Christ!" When you have experienced mistreatment in the ministry by being a woman of God, it isn't the time to walk in un-forgiveness, bitterness and resentment. On the contrary, that is the time to use those experiences as a stepping stone or bridge to catapult you to the next level! Are you willing to do whatever it takes to go to the next level? Then, you go girl! God is with you! He is putting order back in the body of Christ. God is changing the old way of doing things in the church. Unfortunately, some will remain in darkness because they refuse to change.

<u>God has destined women side-by-side with men to rule and reign in the earth.</u>

Chapter 7

Wonderfully and Fearfully Made

It does not matter how you were conceived, the fact is that you are here. God has destined you to win. I have even heard of stories of people that were aborted and they lived to tell the story. The Devil could not kill them! God had a plan for their lives. God has a plan for your life. Get out of the victim mentality! Stop receiving pressure others have tried to interject on you from their shortcomings.

Be the person God has called you to be. There is none like you with the same handprint. You are wonderfully and fearfully made by God.

God has a path that is laid out for us. From the time that you were conceived in your mother's womb; to the time that you were born into this world; unto the time that you go home to be with the Lord.

What path are we going to take? The path that God has laid out for us? A path of destiny to win? Our own path? Or, the path that the Devil has laid out for us?

Just like you have a manufacturer that makes a particular product, you don't ask another manufacturer who doesn't make that particular product how to fix something they've never fixed. It's the same thing with us. How can you ask someone else to fix you with all of your issues? And, they aren't the one who created you. No, instead you go to God the creator of heaven and earth. Ask him to restore you. He is able to tell you everything that there is to know about you, what part of you that needs to be fixed, and why it needs to be repaired. You won't find the answer in self-help books, but God can fix everything that is broken in our lives. I am not saying don't seek professional help if you need professional help such as a psychologist or psychiatrist. Please go because God can use them to bring healing to you, as well.

Wonderfully and Fearfully Made

1. sculp·ture/ ˈskəlpCHər/

Verb: Make or represent (a form) by carving, casting, or other shaping techniques.

Noun: The art of making two- or three-dimensional representative or abstract forms, esp. by carving stone or wood or by casting metal or plaster.

When we think about an artist that makes sculptures. She takes her time to find the most superior material if she wants to make a piece with quality material. She will search for the best and not settle for the cheapest material available to make this exquisite piece of art worth millions of dollars.

He doesn't just throw a few pieces of clay together, smash them and say, "That's it, it's made." But, he takes his time with planning and precisely measuring its dimensions and details to the design, color, shape, size, and what type of art piece that it is required. What is the purpose of this piece of art, who was it made for, where will it go, will it be in a glass or crystal case? Will it be displayed in museums throughout the world or Europe? What type of people will most likely purchase this type of artwork?

Will clients be people from the entertainment field such as athletes, housewives, entrepreneurs, actors, etc…?

What intricate details will I place on this exquisite piece of artwork? Then, you would take your time making, molding, and forming each piece of it being transformed from a lump of clay to this million-dollar piece work of art.

The Father thinks of us in even a greater level of detail and care for us: The color of our skin, eyes, hair, lips, mouth, ears, nose and body. Our Heavenly Father is concerned about; where we would live, who we will marry, how many children if any children we would have, our occupation. Would we be the CEO of a world-wide Fortune 500 company, owner, an educator, lawyer, doctor, in the five-fold ministry? Will we speak before thousands or millions for the Lord? What is our purpose and destiny?

We are God's piece of handcrafted artwork, unique hand-picked, formed with a plan in mind, God's plan and purpose. We are unique, special, and God loves each and every one of us dearly. The love of God is far greater than the love that any human offers. It far surpasses our minute minds.

God himself is the master builder, which has the blue print on our DNA, and how we were made to function in His kingdom.

I Corinthians 12:12-18 says,

"For as the body is one and has many members, but all the members of that one body, being many, are one body, so also is Christ. For by one Spirit we were all baptized into one body—whether Jews or Greeks, whether slaves or free—and have all been made to drink into one Spirit." For in fact the body is not one member but many. If the foot should say, "Because I am not a hand, I am not of the body," is it therefore not of the body?

And if the ear should say, "Because I am not an eye, I am not of the body," is it therefore not of the body? If the whole body were an eye, where would be the hearing? If the whole were hearing, where would be the smelling?

But now God has set the members, each one of them, in the body just as He pleased."

Who are you, which one of these body parts are you, where do you fit in the body of Christ?

You are unique in who you are so be you and nobody else. There may be people that like to imitate you because they like you. But there is not another you in this world. You are special and unique and your part in the body makes it complete!

One of my favorite movies is the 1946 classic, *"It's a Wonderful Life,"* starring Jimmy Stewart as the failed businessman, George Bailey. This holiday movie takes a hard look at George's life and how drastic things would've changed if he weren't born.

George was at the end of his rope and wanted to kill himself because of many things that transpired in his life. The businessman was at rock bottom in his life because he'd given up on his own dreams after helping everyone else throughout the years. God sent an Angel, Clarence Odbody (Henry Travers) to earth. Clarence takes George on a journey, showing him how valuable he was, and how many lives George affected for the good. The Angel also showed George that if he weren't born, he wouldn't have saved his brother from drowning.

Men and women of God you are needed! You are priceless! God thought of you so much that He sent His only Son to stand in the gap for you and pay the price for all your sins, think of that. He loved you and me so much he laid down his life, so that we can be free and live in victory.

I have seen, and am aware of people wanting to be like other people: because they see them as this incredible person. Well, we have to know that we are somebody in Christ. We must know who we are in Him. We are credible in Christ – how about that!

Chapter 8

Victories in Overcoming Life's Obstacles

As a young girl, Cynthia, knew she would be married one day. She was specific in her prayer requests to God. She wanted the type of husband, who was a man with a heart after God. He would treat her as the queen that she is as daughter of the most High God. Cynthia would always watch the '70s "Brady Bunch" TV family show as a little girl. So, she wanted to be like the three boys and three girls on the show and have a housekeeper like Alice (Anne B. Davis). But as Cynthia grew up and matured, her mind was changed and her heart's desire was to have a boy and girl. Cynthia got married to her Godly man and she was employed in corporate America making good money. Soon, she desired to have a child.

However, a doctor discovered Cynthia had fibroids in her uterus the size of grapefruits, which caused excruciating pain. At times, when she walked, she'd stop, and bend over because of throbbing pain and discomfort. The doctor told her that it would be difficult to have a baby because of the fibroids. Nevertheless, Cynthia and her husband stood for several years before the manifestation came.

At the age of 40, Cynthia got pregnant and starting seeing an OB/GYN. The doctor responded with, "You are at high-risk for pregnancy. It is not safe for you to have a baby because of the fibroids that are in your uterus." Cynthia told the doctor, "I appreciate your time that it took for you to go to school to practice medicine, I appreciate the knowledge that you have, but I trust God, who is my great physician." She believed God! And no diagnosis from any doctor would change her faith.

Cynthia attended her first trimester prenatal visits. The doctor said everything was fine, until she went into her second trimester at six months when she began to spot. The doctor took her off of work and put her on bedrest. Unfortunately, Cynthia didn't have the revelation of what bedrest was and continued driving and doing errands until a friend of hers told her that bedrest meant exactly that – *bedrest*! At 34 weeks into the pregnancy, Cynthia was hospitalized. Monitors were attached on her and the baby, and she was fed a special diet. Cynthia was also experiencing high blood pressure. The doctor wanted to take the baby, but was concerned about the stage of development of the unborn child. He decided to wait for the baby to develop a few more weeks.

At 38 weeks into the pregnancy, Cynthia returned to the hospital for a C-section. Prior to prepping for surgery, they asked Cynthia if she wanted a tubal ligation. She told the doctor, "No, thank you. I am going to have another child." The doctor said, "Are you sure?" Cynthia responded, "Yes, I am sure." They conducted the C-Section and a beautiful girl was born, whom she named Naomi. Weeks later, the doctor asked Cynthia if she wanted to get on birth control. Again, Cynthia responded with, "No, I am going to have another baby." The doctor tried everything that he could to discourage her into not having another baby. He reminded Cynthia of her medical history of fibroids, preeclampsia and high blood pressure. Cynthia responded to the doctor, "Once again doctor, I am not trying to disrespect you in any way. But, I have a greater physician and He will heal me."

Approximately one and-a-half years later, Cynthia conceived her second child! Cynthia had favor with God and was blessed to have the head doctor of (OB/GYN) as her treating physician. Other women were on a waiting list to see him, and Cynthia passed them all up. The thing about it was that he was not taking any more new patients, but he took her. Her second child was full term with no complications, and weighed 10 pounds and 11 ounces. To God be the glory, she has two healthy children with the husband that she prayed and believed God for!

My Husband's Victory

In the year of 2000, Terry my husband discovered he had a

hernia and went to the doctor for it. The doctor scheduled him for surgery. While in the doctor's office, Terry noticed a diagram of the human throat on an anatomy chart. Terry asked the doctor why his tonsils did not look like the tonsils in the diagram. The doctor examined Terry's throat area externally and said everything was fine. Terry told the doctor that he needs to check his throat again inside, as well. The doctor said what affects the inside will affect the outside of his throat. Terry was persistent in telling him to check it again. It wasn't until checking three times that the doctor discovered a small lump on the outside. He asked Terry to open his mouth so that he could look inside.

Upon looking into his mouth he told Terry that he was going to refer him to an ENT specialist. Within a couple of days, Terry had an appointment with the ENT specialist, the doctor took a biopsy and the results indicated that he had stage 4B carcinoma of the right tonsil and the doctors prognosis was he had only one year to live. Terry looked at me and began to cry. I knew that his thoughts were racing in his mind. I looked at him and said, "You are healed. We are going to stand on the word of God. And say nothing that does not line up with the word of God, we call it bound from your body right now and sent back to the very pit of hell from whence it comes!"

The doctor came back to Terry and gave him his recommendation, which was to have surgery to remove all the cancer, along with radiation. The days and weeks and prior to Terry's surgery were spent in prayer and fasting mode. We were a praying family sought God for our covering. When the day of Terry's surgery arrived, our family waited for 13 hours in the waiting room. The room was buzzing with other families in the same predicament, so I put on the intercessory mantel and prayed for them, as well. Finally, the doctor came out and told us Terry's surgery was successful. They removed all of the cancer.

However, Terry still needed radiation. The real battle had just begun. Terry's treatment was 60 miles from home, and the treatment warranted five days a week for one month. We had to drive a total of

120 miles a day for 30 days. I had to go from full time employment to part-time in order to take my husband to his treatments. By the second week, Terry's radiation treatments were physically wearing me down. Thankfully, others started pitching to help drive Terry to his treatments. Another woman of God made dinner for my whole family for the entire month while Terry underwent treatment. Five years after his treatment, the doctors declared him cancer-free! At the writing of this book, Terry has been cancer-free for 12 years!

When you see my husband you see the healing power of God in manifestation!!!

Chapter 9
Faith

Walking out the plan of God for our lives is a faith walk. I have seen numerous people that are skilled in certain areas achieve great and mighty things for God. But, due to self-doubt and wrongful thinking of themselves, fixated on inner shortcomings and weaknesses, they cancel themselves out from the destiny of what God has for them. Why? God's sons and daughters see themselves as grasshoppers and less than others. It is time to stop that! We must see ourselves as God sees us. We must paint the picture before us to where God is taking us. We must see ourselves taking kingdom territory. God has given us dominion and power in the earth. Genesis 1:26 KJV states, "Then God said, Let us speaking of the Son and Holy Spirit, make man in Our image, according to our likeness: let them speaking of us, have dominion over the fish of the sea, over the birds of the air, and over the cattle, over all the earth and over every creeping thing that creeps on the earth." Verse 27 says, "So God created man in His own image: in the image of God He created him: male and female He created them." Verse 28 says, "Then God blessed them, and God said to them be fruitful and multiply: fill the earth and subdue it; have domino over the fish of the sea, over the birds of the air, and over every living thing that moves on the earth."

<u>Dominion</u>- In Hebrew means *"Rada," a prim root to tread down, to crumble off, come to make to have dominion, prevail against, reign, bear, make to rule over take.*

With all that dominion and power, we have everything that it takes to win and walk out our destinies! We Win! We win in our jobs; we win in our ministries; we win in our marriages; we win in our relationships with others; we win with our businesses; and we win in our endeavors! Glory to God we are on the winning team! With the tools we use, how can we lose? What tools are we talking about? The word of God is the most important tool. Applying its principles to our everyday life will impact our life and those around us. We influence others by our lives.

I recently attended a dear friend of mine's homegoing service, where this woman read a poem called, "The Dash." What are we doing with our life from the time we're born, all in-between the dash until we go to glory? Are we making a difference around those within our sphere of influence in a positive way? I pray the answer is yes. We can change the lives of others in a good way for the glory of God. We have a choice to obey God and step out in Faith. We have a choice to speak and declare the word of God over our lives and loved ones. We have a choice to put action to our faith, and we have a choice to receive everything the Father has for us by faith. I have a question for you. What are you going to do with all the word that is in you? There is someone out there that needs you. Yes, with everything that you've experienced.

Come on, let's be honest. We know God has really brought us to where we are today. If God had not intervened in some of our lives we wouldn't be here today.

I know some of you may say I am only twenty-plus years, what can I say to someone? You have a lot to say, man or woman of God. The fact you are reading this book tells me that you want better for your life. Even if you are doing well right now, you can always do better. You are destined to win! Some of you reading this book are fifty-plus years, and you are in a good place. You have a lot to impart to this next generation. They need the wisdom that we've obtained over the years. We can share with them the right guidance so they won't have to undergo the same obstacles, brick walls and issues that we experienced through ignorance.

It doesn't matter how young or how old you are, you can make a difference in your generation or even in others. I know you may have heard the old saying that, "age is only a number." Well, there is a little truth to that, and that truth is we can learn something from everybody even a child. Have you ever observed a small child with their parent? He is so trusting, when mommy says that she is going to do something for him. He takes it at face value. "Mommy said it, and I believe it."

Well, we should be the same way with our Heavenly Father, if He says, it then we should believe it. And, that settles it. There are times when I think of the children of Israel and how God delivered them from Pharaoh. Consider how God opened up the Red Sea, and they walked through it on dry ground. I think about how there were no sick or feeble people. I think about how their shoes did not wear out; and about how God provided Manna for them that had all the nutrients that they needed to survive. And, they still murmured and complained. Wow! That's kind of hard to believe when they were there and actually witnessed the manifestation of God's power! God said to me, "They still do the same today, even after I have delivered them over and over again: when I have healed them of physical challenges; when I healed their marriage; when I healed their children; when I saved their home from being taken away from them; and when I blessed them with that job that they prayed for. I've delivered them from the drug addiction and they told me if I delivered them from this situation that they will serve me."

I believe it hurts the heart of God when we don't trust Him like a little child. Proverbs 3:5 (NLT) says, "Trust in the Lord with all your heart, do not depend on your own understanding." Verse 6 says, "Seek His will in all you do, and He will direct your paths." So when we trust Him first; don't yield ourselves or depend on our own self in a matter; don't depend on our own understanding in a matter; seek Him first in a matter, then, He will direct our steps that we make, and we will not slip or fall. Our steps are steady and founded on a sure foundation, which is His word. God's word is the living word of God; the healing word of God; the delivering word of God; the saving word of God, and the casting out of devils word of God. The word of God that we speak and believe in our heart that it will surely come to pass of what God has spoken over our life.

3 John 2 (NLT) says, "Dear friend, I am praying that all is well with you and that your body is as healthy as I know your soul is."

(New Spirit-Filled Bible, NLT) says, "Beloved, I pray that you may prosper in all things and be in health, just as your soul prospers."

He is the God that wants us to prosper in every area of our lives, marriage, jobs, business, school, church, ministry, life. With NOTHING LACKING, NOTHING MISSING, and NOTHING BROKEN.

God wants us prospering in our whole, complete man: spirit, soul and body.

We are tri-part beings: spirit, soul and body. We have a will, mind, and emotions, which comprise our soul man and our spirit man, which is the real you – the one that needs to be born again.

John 3:1-7 clearly illustrates and explains that in order for us to walk out our destiny and our true purpose as God intended, we must be born again. If you can truly say, "I never have done that before. I want to be born again. I realize that I have been doing things on my own, and in my way. I want to make a change and be a part of God's kingdom, and walk out my God-given destiny. Then, repeat the following prayer.

"Dear God, I come to you in the name of Jesus. I believe in your word, where you said whoever comes to you, you will not cast them out, but take them in. You also said in your word, according to Romans 10:9-10. If I confess with my mouth and believe in my heart that God has raised Jesus from the dead, I will be saved. I believe with my heart, and I confess with my mouth right now. Jesus come into my heart and become the Lord of my life. I confess my sins right now and ask you to forgive me. Now, I want to thank you for forgiving me. I am now a new person in you. I have been born again."

If you just prayed that prayer welcome to the family of God! The angels in heaven are rejoicing over one sinner that repents. Repent means to have a change of heart and a change of mind, to make a complete turn around and go in the right direction.

When we were in elementary school, we learned basic math. We learned how one plus one equals two (1 + 1 = 2). That's simple right? Well, it is that simple in understanding that God is in the multiplication business in the lives of his people that obey Him. Mark 5:1-11 (NLT).

One day, while Jesus was preaching along the Sea of Galilee shores, great crowds pressed toward Him. The crowd was excited to hear the word of God, but Jesus needed more space. Jesus noticed fishermen had left two empty boats at the water's edge. The fishermen were washing their nets nearby. Stepping into one of the boats, Jesus asked Simon Peter, the owner, to push it out into the water. Jesus sat in the boat and taught the crowds from there. When he had finished speaking, he said, "Simon, go out where it is deeper and let down your nets and you will catch many fish." "Master," Simon replied. "We worked hard all last night and didn't catch a thing. But if you say so, we'll try again."

This time their nets were so full that they began to tear! A shout for help brought their partners in the other boat, and soon both boats were filled with fish and on the verge of sinking. When Simon Peter realized what had happened, he fell to his knees before Jesus and said, "oh, Lord, please leave me. I'm too much of a sinner to be around you." For he was awestruck by the size of their catch, as were the other's with him. His partners, James and John, the sons of Zebedee, were so amazed.

We see how the multiplication factor was in force. Peter gave from his sustenance (his boat), allowed Jesus to use it to minister to the crowds of people.

And Simon Peter's fishing business, along with those who partnered with him skyrocketed to another dimension. Let's think about that for a minute. Simon worked all night long, and didn't catch anything. This was his livelihood, where he received his income. It doesn't say, but, perhaps, Simon Peter was feeling discouraged and frustrated after working long hours without receiving anything for his efforts. But on the contrary, Simon Peter's manifestation was closer than he imagined! Jesus was right there to bless him exceedingly, abundantly even more than he could even ask or think. There are many of you while reading this book, have been doing everything correct. Although it may look like nothing is happening, and nothing has changed in your situation. Perhaps, even what you've believed God for doesn't appear like it's turned. Don't give up! Your reward is right there! One more step, one more minute, one more day and the manifestation is here! Now! Aren't you glad that you persevered? Aren't you glad that you didn't give up? Aren't you glad you didn't quit? I'm glad that we didn't and are walking in the promises of God!

If you missed it, don't worry: get back on track for God is on your side. We win: our course has been predestined for us. Stay connected to Jesus and you will stay on course with the Master's plan!

Chapter 10
The Multiplication Factor

When Jesus, gave His life for us, there was multiplication that took place. Let's think about it. Jesus started out with 12 disciples (Apostles) The names of The Twelve are listed in 4 places in **The Bible** (Matthew 10:2-4, Mark 3:16-19, Luke 6:12-19, Acts 1:13) with some minor differences due to the various uses of first, family, or nicknames at different times.- Simon, Andrew, James (son of Zebedee), John, Phillip, Bartholomew, Thomas, Matthew, James (son of Alpheus), Thaddeus, Simon, and Judas Iscariot. From The Twelve to Millions of believer's in the world today!

The multiplication is still intact today as many more receive Jesus Christ as their Lord and Savior. God keeps on adding and adding to our life as we seek His kingdom first; as we seek His counsel first; as we trust Him with all our heart; and we don't lean to our own understanding, but instead all of our ways, we acknowledge Him and He will direct your steps and make your steps are sure (Proverbs 3:5). God wants to bless us exceedingly, abundantly above more than we can even ask or think, according to the power that worketh in us. We have the power and the ability in us to obtain wealth, so God can establish His covenant in us. I am in covenant with the almighty God. How about you? You see, when we are in covenant with God, that means everything that He has we have and the same for us. Whatever we have He possesses. Now, when you know the character of our Creator who created the heaven and earth, when He says He's going to do something in your life, you can rest assured that He will come through for you. Everything that you give to Him he takes multiples of it and gives it back to us.

When we say Lord this is everything that I have and I give it back to you. He takes it and multiplies it thirty-, sixty-, or one-hundred fold. Is that not multiplication? A husband and wife join together and the wife conceives: that's one plus one equals three ($1 + 1 = 3$). That beautiful boy or girl that God blessed you with is a multiplication that only God create!

Chapter 11
Worship

Oxford Dictionary-*"Worship means the feeling or expression of reverence and adoration for a deity."* The Webster's dictionary say's it like this, *"to love, admire, or esteem devotedly."*

God created us to worship Him. There are angels in heaven who are assigned to worship Him 24-hours a day saying, "Holy, Holy, Holy." That's what they do all day long. Worship comes from the depth within the very recesses of your heart, the core. Your heart or you could say your spirit man, which is the real you that was born again longs and hungers to worship God. Having a love affair relationship with the Lord is longing to spend time with Him. You long to get in his presence as much as you can. I know many of you have to get your children up and prepare their breakfast and lunches, along with praying for them before sending them off to school. If you are married there may be different things that you do with each other before you are off and running before you leave the house. One thing I have found out in my own life is that when I put God first in my everyday schedule, my day flows a lot better than when I miss my early morning, prayer and devotion time with the Lord. Here are some things to implement into your life on a daily basis- When you get up in the morning, you get dressed before you go outside right? Well, just like we get dressed daily, we need to be clothed spiritually.

You may ask, "How do I do that." I'm glad you asked. I am going to show you how.

Romans 13:14 (Amplified) says, "But clothe yourself with the Lord Jesus Christ (The Messiah), and make no provision for (indulging) the flesh (put a stop to thinking about the evil cravings of your physical nature) to (gratify its) desires (lusts)."

When we clothe ourselves with the Lord Jesus Christ, we make a declaration over ourselves by saying, "Father, I clothe myself with the Lord Jesus Christ. I thank you that greater is He that is in me than he that is in the world. I thank you that I have the mind of Christ. I hold the thoughts, feelings, and purposes of your heart. I hold fast to my confession of faith, for I walk by faith and not by sight. Thank you that as I go throughout my day, that I am conscious that you are here with me. I will not say or do anything that will grieve your spirit in me (Holy Spirit) this day. I thank you for it in Jesus' name."

Some people like to play worship music while they are praying, I pray without it for the most part at home because it is so early in the morning that I do not want to wake my family. When I pray corporately at church or at a ministry event, I like to have some anointed worship on while I am praying. Corporate prayer and corporate worship is different than your own personal devotional time with the Lord. When you are alone with the Lord, you can let it go, and worship as loud as you choose. Play your music at the volume you want and within reason of consideration toward your family members. The main thing is that we are alone with the Lord.

There are numerable aspects of worship in the life of the believer. When we live a life of worship unto the Lord, signs, wonders, and miracles manifest in our life.

Let's explore another story in the Bible. In the book of Acts 16:16-32, Paul was on his way to pray, when he's followed by a slave girl operating in a spirit of divination (psychic). Along the way, she says to Paul and comrades, "These are the men of the Most High God. They announce to you the way of Salvation." I have a question for you. Was she speaking the truth? The answer is yes, but she was operating under the influence of a demonic spirit.

When you read this you will see that Paul didn't cast out the devil right away but he waited. It says in the word that this situation occurred for several days. It was only after Paul got annoyed and fed up with this woman who was demon-possessed, that he spoke to that demon and told it to leave. It had to flee because of the authority that Paul walked in. This young girl that was a slave made her owners a lot of money, and when their profit was gone because the demon was cast out, they grabbed Paul and Silas. The two were put in the market place jail, where their trials were held. Up until now, Paul and Silas were ministering to the community and attending daily prayer, while this demon was manifesting itself through this slave girl. Now, here they are in the market place, and brought before magistrates, under false accusations of causing confusion and encouraging practices and customs, which are unlawful as Romans. A big crowd gathered around and instigated the confusion even more. The rowdy crowd not only tore the clothes from Paul and Silas, and but also beat them with rods. Unfortunately, they were they were stripped publicly and humiliated. Roman guards put Paul and Silas in the market's inner prison cell. Later that night, something miraculous happened.

Instead of whining and complaining, Paul and Silas began to pray and sing hymns to God at about midnight. Now, keep in mind they weren't praying or singing in a low voice. These two were singing at a volume, where other prisoners were listening, while they were singing. All of a sudden, a great earthquake shook the very foundations of the prison, causing the doors to open. Everyone's shackles were broken. The revelation is that when we worship the Father in the midst of deep persecution; in the midst of doing the right thing; and getting attacked by others; in the midst of the most trying time in your life; as we begin to praise and worship Him; God will shake the very foundation of that trial and storm; the shackles that have had you bound for so many years are broken off of you now in Jesus' name.

<u>Prophetic Word of the Lord</u>
"As You have sought my face, as You have persevered through the storm, and You purposed in your heart, I am going to worship you Lord. I am going to magnify You Lord. I don't understand what I am going through right now, but Lord I trust you, and I glorify you right now. You are worthy Lord, to receive all the glory, and the honor, and

the praise. I am doing a shifting of things. I am rearranging things in your life. For some of you, there are many things out-of-order; out-of-order from the kingdom's way of doing things. But this day, I am rearranging the things that caused you to fall short from my desire for you and your life. My desire is for you to overcome in every area of your life. Put on your new garment, shred and destroy the old garment that represents the old you. Yes, you say, "But Lord, I am born again." And I say, "Yes, I know, but there is more than just your salvation in me: much more than you can even ask or think. Promotion to some of you: refining fire for others. Unless you come to me, and worship Me in My holiness, you will not receive everything that I desire for you to have. For, you see, mysteries, are unlocked in My presence; mysteries are revealed in My presence; come before Me this day and worship me in My holiness saith the Lord!"

I will seek Your face Lord

I love You Lord!

I will worship You for who You are

- <u>El Shaddai</u> (Lord God Almighty)
- <u>El Elyon</u> (The Most High God)
- <u>Adonai</u> (Lord, Master)
- <u>Yahweh</u> (Lord, Jehovah)
- <u>Jehovah Nissi</u> (The Lord My Banner)
- <u>Jehovah-Raah</u> (The Lord My Shepherd)
- <u>Jehovah Rapha</u> (The Lord That Heals)
- <u>Jehovah Shammah</u> (The Lord Is There)
- <u>Jehovah Tsidkenu</u> (The Lord Our Righteousness)
- <u>Jehovah Mekoddishkem</u> (The Lord Who Sanctifies You)
- <u>El Olam</u> (The Everlasting God)
- <u>Elohim</u> (God)
- <u>Qanna</u> (Jealous)
- <u>Jehovah Jireh</u> (The Lord Will Provide)
- <u>Jehovah Shalom</u> (The Lord Is Peace)
- <u>Jehovah Sabaoth</u> (The Lord of Hosts)

Chapter 12
Prayer

In this chapter, I will lay out prayers for you to pray for yourself and others that will open doors of opportunities for walking out your destiny.

Declaration

Father, I come before You this day, worshipping You, and adoring You. Lord, You are worthy to receive all the glory, and honor, and thanksgiving, and praise.

I thank You Lord that you are Jehovah Makkeh in my life; You make and mold me into Your image.

I thank You Lord that You are Jehovah Jireh in my life; I thank You that all my needs are met, according to Your riches and glory in Christ Jesus.

I thank You I walk and operate in the overflow: that I may be a blessing to others wherever I go. I thank You that I am the lender and not the borrower. There is surplus and reserves in my bank account.

When there is a need in the body of Christ, I thank You that I am a conduit in which money flows, and I will be obedient to sow, where You tell me to sow.

You said in your Word in (Amplified version) John 15:7, "If you live in me abide vitally united to me and your words remain in me and continue to live in my heart, that whatever I ask you, it shall be done for me."

I purpose in my heart to abide in You and remain in You on a daily basis. So, Father, I ask that You bless me, and enlarge my territory. I thank You that you are with me, wherever I go, and You keep me from evil so it might not hurt me.

I thank You for opening doors of opportunities, divine connections coming to me now in Jesus name. I thank You that You are raising me up with power, ability, and influence to help someone else.

I thank You that You have given me the ability to obtain wealth and that You may establish your covenant with me. Now in the name of Jesus, I come against every hindering spirit that would try to block my progress. I am what God said that I am, and I will do what God said I will do. I am a champion for the kingdom of God. I have favor with God and man. I am a believer and not a doubter. For, I hold fast to my confession of faith. For, I walk by faith and not by sight. I will not be denied what rightfully belongs to me.

I thank You, Lord that I recover all that was stolen from me. Now, in the name of Jesus, jobs, relationships, money, houses, cars, time, territory, health, opportunities are being restored in the name of Jesus.

Lord I give You the Glory!

I thank You, Lord that I excel in everything that I set my hands to do: whether it's ministry, my career, entrepreneurship, school, business, marriage, parenting, socially, or in relationships. I am a winner. I win.

I am walking out destiny for my life. I am walking out the plan of God for my life. Others that come in contact with me will be compelled to assist me, because I walk in the favor of God, and God is on my side. If God is for me, who can be successfully against me?

My words are seasoned with salt that I will not be at a loss in how to answer any man. I am confident. I am successful. I walk in my rightful, God-given authority, and I walk in the peace of God, which surpasses all understanding.

According to Psalm 37:4, "I delight myself in you, Lord and I thank You. You give me the desires of my heart." Matthew 7:7, "You said in Your word that if I ask it will be given to me, seek and I will find, Lord I am seeking you first, knock I am knocking, Lord, and You said it shall be open to me, So I thank You for every open door that

You have for me that I recognize it and I walk in your perfect timing.

Every blockade and hindrance is annihilated in Jesus' name. I thank You because Your word abides in me. I speak only what You want me to speak so that my angels are dispatched on my behalf: to bring in what I need in the name of Jesus.

When I get up in the morning, the devil and his cohorts are afraid, because I am your child and I am booted and suited with Your word in my mouth! I am representing You, wherever I go. For, I am Your ambassador a dignitary for Your kingdom! Now, I speak to every place in my life that is not bearing good fruit. I thank You, Lord that a reversal has come in my life, and I am a good fruit producer. I affect others for Your kingdom this day. I thank you that this day I am led and directed by Your Spirit. I hear accurately and precisely in Jesus' name.

Prayer for Salvation

Dear God I come to You in the name of Jesus. I believe when You said in Your word, whoever comes to You, You will not cast out. But, You will take me in. You also said according to Your word that if I confess with my mouth the Lord Jesus, and believe in my heart that You raised Jesus from the dead, I will be saved. I receive You, Lord Jesus as my personal Lord and Savior. Come into my heart and become the Lord of my life. I want to thank You for forgiving me of all my sins and healing me in Jesus name. (Romans 10: 9-10)

Prayer for Rededication

Father, You said in Your word in 1 John 1:9, "If I confess my sins, to you, you are faithful and just to forgive me of all my sins, and to cleanse me of all unrighteousness. I ask for forgiveness now and I am coming back to you now in the name of Jesus." I thank You that You are a healing and restoring God and I am being restored right now in Jesus' Name.

Prayer for the Infilling of the Holy Sprit

Father, I come to You in the name of Jesus, just as I received Jesus as my Lord and Savior, I am asking You to fill me with the Holy Spirit with the evidence of speaking in other tongues. I receive it now in the name of Jesus. Acts 1:8; Acts 2: 4; John 14:16, 17, 26; Luke 11:9-13

Outreach in the park

Free Toy giveaway to the poor

Go into all the World and Preach the Gospel!

Me and Hubby chilling

And God Said!

Prayer changes things

Agreement in Prayer

Teaching the Word

Feeding the homeless

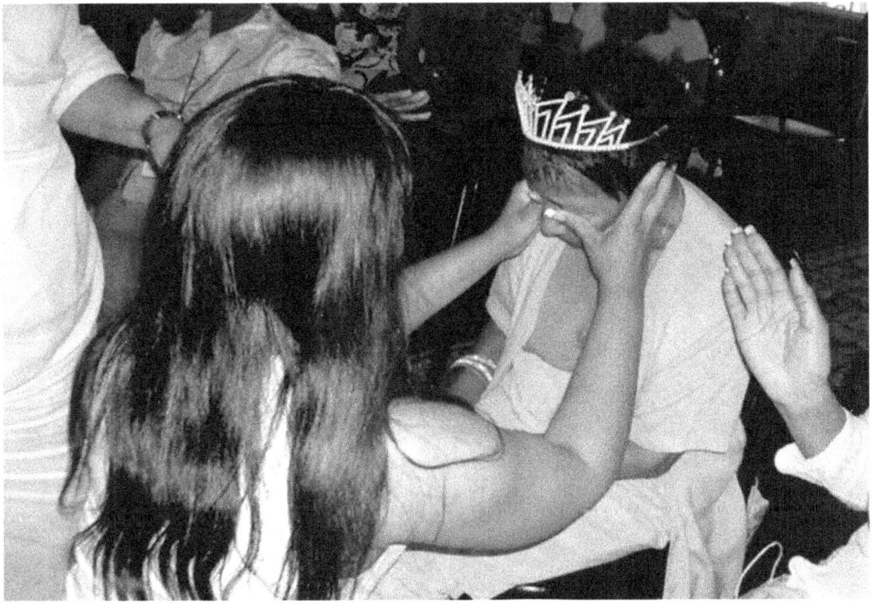

Anointing Mommy

Outreach ministry in the Park

Ministering to the needy

Christmas Outreach

Preaching the Word

Dr. L'Tanya James & Husband, Elder Terry James

Feeding the homeless

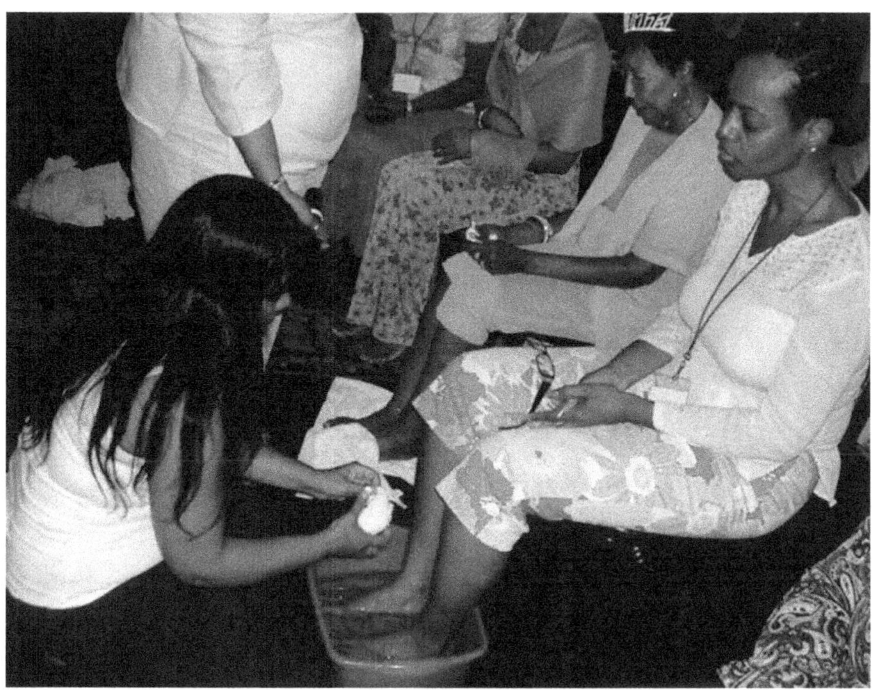

Foot washing service

I will Praise the Lord!

L'Tanya James
Outreach Ministries

Signs and wonders

Jesus is Lord

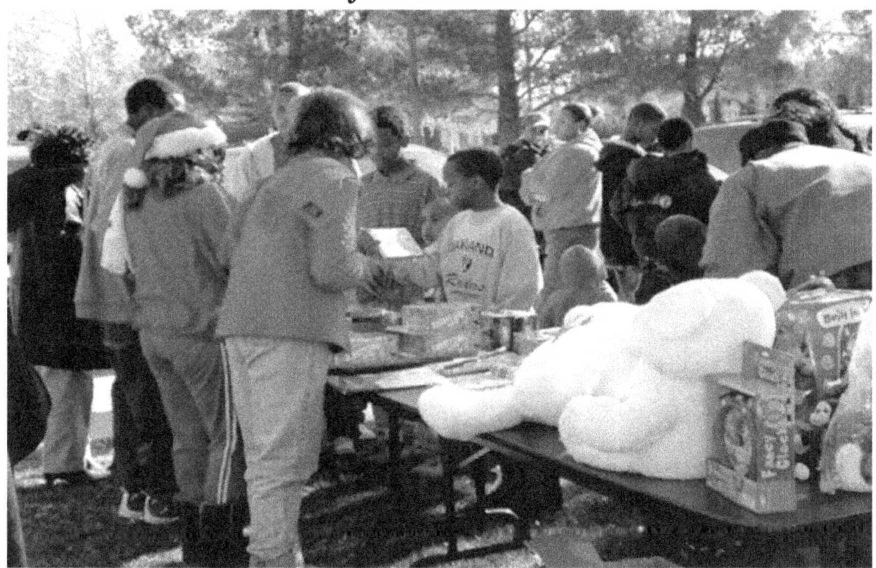

Christmas Toy Giveaway!

Outreach at the Park

Mommie
Ministering at my conference

About the Author

Dr. James has served in ministry for more than 31 years, working as a foundation builder of prayer rooms, prison ministries, dance ministries, women fellowships, Sunday and mid-week services speaker, conference host, youth and women retreats and so much more.

She opened her Outreach Ministry in 2004 where she hit the streets and ministered to the homeless population with free food, clothing and resources and ministered the Gospel in local parks and many people were saved, healed, set-free and delivered. She currently partners with two ministries in Pakistan where she ministers the Word of God via Skype where Healing and Deliverance services take place. Dr. James can be heard every 5th Sunday on the Gospel for the Glory of Jesus Radio Program.

In her church, Living Praise Christian Center, where Dr. Fred L. Hodge and Pastor Linda G. Hodge are Senior Pastors, with locations in Chatsworth, Santa Clarita, and Palmdale, California, she works as a Bible College Instructor and serves as a board member of the newly founded Chamber of Commerce.

She is the business owner of Next Dimension LLC, a business that prepares leaders to reach their potential.

Dr. James is a graduate of Rhema Correspondence Bible College, graduate of American Association of Christian Counselors, graduate of International College of Bible Theology with a Bachelor's Degree in Biblical Studies, received an Honorary Doctorate, Master's Degree in Divinity, and a graduate of Living Praise Christian Institute.

Dr. James and her husband of 32 years have two children, three grandchildren and they reside in Southern, California.

Bibliography

Merriam-Webster's collegiate dictionary, 11th ed., (Springfield: Merriam-Webster, Inc., 2003), s.v. "purpose"

New Spirit-Filled Life Bible, New Living Translation, Hayford, Jack, Thomas Nelson, 2013.

The Oxford Dictionary, The Oxford Thesaurus: American Edition, Oxford University Press, Inc., 1992 "worship"